Alzheimer Poems

Alzheimer Poems

Laurel Brodsley

iUniverse, Inc.
New York Lincoln Shanghai

Alzheimer Poems

iUniverse books may be ordered through booksellers or by contacting:

iUniverse
2021 Pine Lake Road, Suite 100
Lincoln, NE 68512
www.iuniverse.com
1-800-Authors (1-800-288-4677)

ISBN-13: 978-0-595-40885-6 (pbk)
ISBN-13: 978-0-595-85248-2 (ebk)
ISBN-10: 0-595-40885-0 (pbk)
ISBN-10: 0-595-85248-3 (ebk)

Printed in the United States of America

Contents

Who am I?

I have been doing the same things I always do.
Those I can do.
But then, when I can't,
I remember that I can't remember.

The shell of my body
And of my mind, still and aware,
While all around me
People quietly do what they do.
And I do not know how long my doing can last.
I made a wish, a wish to get over it.
I made a wish to join those who have gone there before.
And now I have another wish:
To stay.
But will I stay, flesh and bone with no brain,
An anguish for others who love.

Every day I have to remember who I am.
The teacher, the lover, the daughter and mother.
Whose selves are clearly wrapped around.

A self whose identity is wrapped around in tendrils
And plaques.
If only these plaques could be washed away,
Like a toothbrush scrubbing the brain.

I hover here, with a pause to remember the name,
Entangled in cognitive confusion.
Who am I? The teacher, the lover, the mother,
the child?

Typing at 3 a.m.

What in the world should I be typing at 3 a.m?
Alzheimer's leads to wandering around the house.
My house is too small to get lost.
Perhaps I am hungry at night with hypoglycemia,
Or maybe this is my only private time and place.
My caretakers do not like me to walk around at night.
My husband wants me to go back to bed,
But I don't want to go there.
I feel like I might miss something,
Even though there is nothing to do at 3 a.m.
Yes, I remember now,
But now I lost my thought again.
Now I remember that these words and ideas are ephemeral
Scraps of discordant words
Trying to find…poetry.

A Harsh Future

I feel very sad for my friends and family
They are the ones who will see me decay.
Now I turn to the flowers,
with the dirt between my fingers.
That is something I can do right now…
No, I need someone to drive me to the nursery.
What an irony, the word "nursery"
Where I will be like a "baby" as I go down.
They tell me that at the end stage of Alzheimer's,
I will need care in every way, like a baby.
Well, maybe it won't be that bad, or, I might die first
Nowadays I can still do quite a bit, writing, cooking.
The bad stuff now is blank words.
If I need, I take a person by the hand,
and walk with him until I get the issues completed.

In my little life right now
I am constrained by fears.
While I am doing the things that I can do,
I bring back memories,
I lose some words.
Others return, surround me,
I wish that the future could be more benign.
They are the ones who suffer,
In my case I am both caretaker and caregiver,
First taking care of my body and mind.
My other caregiver is my previous identity,
Who sees everything, whatever I do.
For my family and friends
It would have to be a miracle.
I am patient. I can wait.

Sticky Brain

Today my brain is sticky.
A good brisk walk will help it.
A crisp cold wind unwinds it .
That is how I put myself back.

When I wake up, my brain feels like sticky tape.
An ear, perhaps, bends against the skull.
Then an eye opens, with a little crust.
Then my nose smells the aroma of breakfast,
Instant salivation from bacon sizzling on the grill.
There is a little draft from the window.
Now the kitchen is filled with light,
the clink of cutlery, the voices of family.
By now, the neurons have brought it all together.
Our family, the husband, the cat, all taken care of.
I thank the goodness that surrounds me.

Night

I took a walk, in the dark.
I went a few paces, barefoot.
I felt the cool night, and my back was cold too.
I did not have anything to say.
Just me and my cold chair, just sitting there.
Nearby there are pillows in which I could cuddle.
I liked the cold, crisp air, unlike the stuffy small room.
I do nothing: sit, and watch the moon and stars.
This is where I am, where only the wind changes.
This is a blank, nothing.

And I walked all over the house, around it many times.
The house was quiet, nobody but me.
Maybe the cat knocked something down in our house,
We have cracks all over the place.
This is how I feel,
like my huge coral pieces, nothing.
The door does not open for me.
I told you I feel the stars.
I don't know why I'm so sad and empty.
Tears turned my eyes red.
My computer refuses to acknowledge my pain.

Plaque

I was minding my own business
when black holes shot through my brain,
dendrites covered with gunk,
worse than dental-office floss.
I could not scrape off the film,
or unwind the string of thoughts,
slippery, sliding away
from my comprehension.
There was no relief.
The holes, I thought, were metaphoric.
The MRI was real, or was it just another test?

In the dark

It seems to me that I am in the dark
There is an ordinary dark, the dusk of the end of day,
And there is a mental darkness, where words black out,
Not to return.

There is also the dark of a movie house,
charged with color and sound,
movement of the play.

Then there is the darkness of eyes that cannot focus.
A crack in the sidewalk
A trip and a fall that can kill.

There is the dimming of the eyes, cataracts,
With hopes that that surgery brings back the light.
My mother has only one usable eye.
It must be cherished.

For me, I am scared of the dark.
Even in the house, I am lost
if the lights are not on. My hand reaches out,
fingering objects like a children's game.

My mother Tillie has a blind friend, blind from youth.
He lives a life of friendship, adventure, and taking risks.
I wish I were so courageous.
I wish that I could find comfort in the dark.

I think I have lost my muse.

I think I have lost my muse.
With the worry about my obesity,
I lost my sense of taste.
Perhaps it got lost with too many photos,
or lost from too much thought of wars.
Oh, the days of wonderful beauty are gone,
And the joy and delight of ideas that fly.
I used to slide smoothly into my thoughts,
But now I feel gray, and sad, mired in mud.
Yet, I know that my family is lovely, the sun shines, and birds
    tweet.
But the sadness remains, the loss of joy.
And then sometimes I find laughter with my mommy Tillie.
That should be enough.

My Study

My study is ten by ten.
Blue paisley curtains make the room dark, and small.
One wall is a dark wood panel.
One wall and a ceiling are white.
The rest is covered with books.
How long will it be until I can no longer read them?

The shelves describe what I have done.
The Oxford English Dictionary, two volume edition.
Statistics: when I could not compute that "x" is as the same as
    "y" I knew was in trouble.
Most of the books are for literature.
I read fast.
I skim fast.
I have or had almost all of the great literature in the Western
    world in my head.

I loved to share them with students.
But now, I no longer have students,
and few people care about the great literature of the Eastern or
    the Western world

We are now in a culture of illiteracy
But it doesn't matter, since nobody cares.
How many inflections can a person say, if the only word used is
    "Hey!"

I am lonely
I miss my friends:
I miss the world of great literature,
and my friends: Keats, who understood my sensuality,
And I miss Blake, my pal for his brevity,

And I miss irony from Donne, which I no longer have,
And my Hopkins, for the miracle of dappled things.

And left for the last, my buddy Will,
who helped me burrow into his words,
an adventure in every phrase with a shake of the stick.

Getting Lost

Should I take the pill, or not?
If so, will I be different?
They say I will have a year.
If I don't take the pill,
Will I become different?
What shall I do with my year,
Of slow or fast degeneration,
Or a year of further frustrations?

A year of travel perhaps?
A year of getting lost in new places?
Or a year of lost words?

I will find a way to not get lost.
I will wave my silk flowers
And hum on my harmonica.
I will wave the flowers for Sight
And the harmonica for Sound.

But who would let me hum in a museum?
Or whistle in an art gallery?

And can my family keep me safe?
They fear that if I walk away,
I will be confused,
And I may abandon them even if I sit still.
Even if I sit still.

Scenes Behind my Eyelids

*They told me that the medicine Aricept could give me
unusual dreams*

What a wonderful gift!
Every evening, I can put on a show of my choosing.
Sometimes a play, costumes and all.

Then, the screen flickers, the screen in my mind.
I shoot off fireworks, high in the sky.

Sometimes they flicker and fade in the night,
Sometimes reform and dissolve.
And I see washes of colors, plants from my home.

I recreate images I have recently seen.
Then there is something old, a black and white photo, fading
　　away,
As if I could reach out and touch memories.
And I see family photographs.
My brain has recorded all of this,
And this beauty, dancing on neurons, re-creating my life.

Then, most unexpectedly, the medicine kicks in.
What gorgeous colors like a kaleidoscope!
I look up, I see the lights of cathedral windows each evening,
With brilliant colors of glass.

Then, there is a sheet of color, an intense blood red,
Entwined with the blackness,
And deep blue figures, like ghosts,

With black and blue patterns, stirring and swirling,
Like an old fashioned lava lamp, what fun for my brain.

What a lovely gift, even if it is a side effect from some lousy
disease.

Going Slow

Why does my life now go so slowly, like molasses?
Appropriate for food, or for plants, or for talking to grass.
I have not talked about this before,
but time has no part of my brain now.

I know my birthday, yes, May 9th 1939.
The other days, months, may no longer have meaning.
But when I bring my body to various places the mind interferes.
People ask me about times and dates.
So far my birthday is intact as May 9th, 1939

In the house I have been watching how far I can go.
Now my time is slow.
I have 50 minutes to take care of my day,
for my mind skittles off to unknown emptiness.
I am almost ready to go, but frequently there is the dash to the
    toilet:
The monster of irritable bowel throws me into my world again.

So again I don't know how far I can go.
The worst is staring at a house, or a street name,
And if I dare to turn around, I am at risk of being lost.

Tillie, my mother, is getting slower and slower herself,
so I follow her.
But she is totally lucid.
Not me.
Tillie's slowness is only physical;
Mine is a slowness of a deteriorating brain.

Rocks and Worms

In my garden there is a bed of weeds and rocks.
I pick up every one.
This becomes a meditation for me.
I pick up each stone, one by one.
I crumble clod or earth.
Soon I see the worms which look up with blind heads.
I see the wiggles and slimy things.
I was taught that worms are needed for a healthy garden.
But this is about me, picking up, rock by rock.
I pick up things that are not worms or rocks or roots.
I am the worm, pressing in the earth, turning one direction or
　　another.
I am on the ground, feeling the cool earth,
And one by one I make several mounds of rocks.
Feeling happy, moving back and forth.
Finally the rocks are done.
Some rocks turn out to be clods of dry earth.
I do it myself, sitting on the dirt,
The sun gently caressing my cheeks.
This is the season of February and the sweet sun.

Hummingbirds

On a very hot summer day
Two hummingbirds, with flashes of red,
Came to the porch where I sat.
I love the colors of the birds and the flowers,
And now I have two hummingbirds to watch,
Each bird flashing different colors.
They hover and zoom, hover and zoom,
In and out of the bougainvilleas,
And hover over a dish of water
In which some blossoms float.

Lulu the strange cat

She was very pretty, with a gray and white pattern.
She was so cute, but there was something wrong.
Our other cats avoided her.
We thought she was sick,
But the Vet said she had no disease,
And she was so very sweet.

I think she had a cognitive problem.
She never talked to me, or anyone.
She didn't purr and she didn't groom herself,
She never licked her feet,
She never responded as a proper cat should.
Physically she was fed,
And she ate when she got hungry.
It was sad, she just could not be a proper cat.
While our other two cats frolicked around,
She had no interest in the garden,
So filled with cat fun like butterflies, and runs and jumps.
She just curled her cute gray body,
And seemed to not have any interest in her life.
She sat, and sat, and sat.

Then there was the issue of keeping her,
As our other cats knew there was something wrong,
And they avoided her.
What a sad story.
We took Lulu back to the Pound,
Where she may find a little old lady
Who likes to sit, and sit, and sit.

Persimmons

The persimmon is a round red fruit.
The persimmon changes as it grows.
First it is firm, glistening like a Christmas ball.
Then it softens a little, as if tentative, not quite sure
What to do when surrounded with other red fruits.
Then it releases a tough skin, revealing its power
To do what it wants. Then it softens, quietly,
Like so many other fruits of red, like apples.
Now it is normal, hard with thick skin, like other fruits.
And then there is the hat.
First the fruit is like an apple, but not as sweet,
And then it softens, and the inside is the color of fresh blood,
And the texture is slippery, as of the insides of the living body.
Finally I cut around the fruit.

Touch

There is so much beauty in a touch
The warm baby grasps with her tiny finger.
The old man, he too grasps,
But his is cold, like a withered frozen stick
But now I welcome my weathered pair of jeans,
From my youth, when I rolled up my cuff.
The rolled stiff dark jeans,
that mark power for the strong young men,
Wooing the charming girls, with pierced ears
And rolls of soft skin, exposed for love

Turtle

This time the water in the YMCA pool was sleek with no
    bubbles.
I was like a turtle with its carapace.
The water just sits there, smooth and blue
And I embrace a noodle of plastic foam.

Each swimmer has his place: fast lanes for exercise
Another for bobbing up and down and diving.
And for looking out of the window covered with trees.
I am in this watery place, surrounded with plants and trees.
Studio City is a wonderful little town, with a thriving main
    street.
It seems so safe, but the seniors still drift into pain and losses.
And my turtle carapace is not very hard.
But it will be there to help me for what I need.

Women at the Pool

The old masters would love these women,
Their dimpled thighs, their rolling heaves of belly fat,
So soft and pink

And the men who love them,
burying their faces their in their breasts
Warm, full, mothers all.

Then, the young girls, slicing through the watery lanes,
Arms cutting through the water,
They do not make a ripple, their limbs are graceful, muscled,
Pleased with their prowess,
Rubbing oils on their smooth limbs.

We, the older women, with our cellulite, bent with arthritis,
We are also the survivors of the deep.

Leaves and Skin

This is a season of degeneration.
The leaves turn from red to brown,
Then they are soggy and then crisp,
And then the crisp turns into wrinkles.
This happens on our bodies too, the crinkles turn to dust.
And at the end, into the final dust.
I would like to have the beauty of the leaves
And the beauty of the elders' skin, like powder.
They have their own beauty, I honor them
with the blue veins and mottled splashes
of the hand, and the hand is cold.

Yosemite

Today is a time not of poetry but of reminiscence.
When did I go to Yosemite last?
I thrilled with rainbow mists, winding paths,
times of snow or dry brilliant skies.

Times of fires,
obliterating the gorgeous scenes
of rock and tree and sky.

How many times, the gentle meadows, the regal deer?
How many the raging waterfalls?
And as usual the swimming pool.

This is the most beautiful park of them all,
And at night we lay in the meadow
And looked up and counted shooting stars.

And one day my 5-year-old son, looking up at El Capitan,
said "That must be the face of God"

The Sequoia Tree

Yesterday we drove through the Sequoia forest
To visit the trees that I love so much.
The first thing I do is stand back a while, to see the underbrush,
To note that a new path was created,
With a zig-zag pattern, lightly sloping for the disabled.
I thought of my disabilities, I would feel like a gangster if I
    stepped off the path.
Instead, I found a bench, and I stretched out, tilting back my
    head,
To raise my soul up to the canopy of the trees,
Where my eye gazes up and up and up,
Past the shrubs, the trees, and into the sky.
Then, already the comfort is happening, the joy of the master
    sooths my soul.
Now for the ritual hug.
I reach out, but I can't touch him on the other side, since he is
    10 feet in diameter.
From his rings of life, I honor him.
And then,
I come up to my tree, I caress him, and we play music on his soft,
    spongy bark.
The lovely boom and bam, cupping my hands,
Slapping with glee, singing with the birds.
And he and I become a drum, whose notes had come from the
    millennium
The boom of his beautiful red body, this gentle master of the
    wilderness.
The next ritual is the trunk, and the tissue of his bark.
I peel maybe a thin slice, but I leave that alone.
Instead, here comes my favorite part: the music.

These giant masters have survived flood and fire, man and
lightning.
But some have succumbed to men, and eventually they fall.
Perhaps my sequoia will make a nice chair for a patio, or a
beautiful wooden bowl.
I would like to know that he is useful as well as beautiful, this
master of mine.

The Coral Reef

I snorkeled around in the forest of coral
In the reef off the Baby Beach at Lahaina, Maui,
I saw a huge round coral with golden lights.
As I moved around, I saw that there was a pathway
leading to another huge coral.
And I became a fish two feet above the sand.
I wanted to stay forever with my fish body and the sand.
And I found that the water had a road between the corals,
And then the road stopped, suddenly,
So I turned to another place of color and beauty,
With fish of stripes of green and gold.
This was a world of water,
Turning and twisting and buoyant out of this world,
A world so precious for me.
With my body so heavy I live in another world.

Paradise in Maui

Now I can be in Paradise.
Just a few steps into the water,
And there I am, waist high, warm water,
Clear enough to see corals and fish.
I walk with ease, everything is safe.
This is the beach for the babies.
Ironically this beach is best for me.
I am like a child, on the sunlit sands.
The sunset is luminous,
Orange and red blazing at the end of the day.

Fish mate

Now I have nearly drowned, like you,
We can talk about
The love of water.
I wish I would be with you, a fish mate.
Once I innocently started
going down,
I would like to have a fish mate to care for
Among some gorgeous coral reefs.
I would swim with you in Hawaii
And off I go again there.
You would take the big gasp over and over
And I would go down, with 30 minutes of air.
Could I be a mermaid?
Today I've practiced side strokes to swim with legs together.
A swim should be a shared event.
I found other poets who love the water,
Though in the safety of a pool.

New York Shimmers

I had a feeling about nature on this trip:
I especially wanted to see a pink tree,
and a white tree full of shimmering flowers.
And along with the waving grass in Central Park
the trees were in constant movement, tremulous.

The pink cheeks of cold brisk skin,
And the warmth of the shimmering sun
And the dancing waters at the Central Park fountain
In the boating lake, the little waves of toy white sailboats,
Responding to the wind's waves in the water.

Always the sky, the dust motes reminding me of the big hole,
While church windows have slants that cross the beauty,
Creating a kaleidoscope.
The low roar of the subway under the street,
the running of children at play,
and the motes of particulates, shining.
This is New York, a city that never sleeps.
But we did stop, in the museums while the brain itself glows
Watching the spirituality of the art.

This was a most wonderful vacation,
with loving friends and new discoveries.
The Metropolitan, and the Frick, and the Cloisters,
Where rich men provided these marvels for all.

The Concert Bass Viol

The bass viol, over six feet tall, almost ready for basketball
But no, the call is not for the ball.
The call is for beauty, the rich colors and tones of the wood
From which the bass viol was born.

They are in the back row again.
With growling twangs and robust booms
The bass viol players stand in line.

They have little to do, most of the time.
I am watching them, moving with their strong shoulders,
These tall young and old men,
with strong wrists, and finger joints, and strength to
hoist such a heavy burden, for our pleasure.

We wonder what kind of person is the bass player?
Does he hide behind this wooden box, six foot high instrument?
They have strength to pull those metallic strings.
Then they are home, in the back line again,.

Then...
After the concert, the bass player gently places the bass
In its crypt-like case, not for death, but ready for joy.

The violin

The violin can be carried everywhere,
Tucked under the arm.
She is light, she has a silky gloss,
As delicious as a red tabby cat.
She is precious.
She can be very expensive.
She is a work of art.
She is very difficult to play well.
The body has to twist in a strange posture.
The orchestra needs her
with her sound like a human voice.
She is like a woman, with her curves and edges,
her long hair, that must be pulled back and forth.
She is exquisite, her beautiful voice can bring us to tears.

Old Jeans

Still the jeans cling to the skin, formed from all those years.
A stroke of the hand, caressing the cloth
Softened from years of wearing jeans.
The cloth tells a story.
The first jeans of youth, rolled up,
Boyishly. Even the girls do it.
The cloth hard and stiff
With the first wash.
Later the creases smooth out,
The colors change.
Then there will be creases.
The color changes, from dark blue to blue-gray,
From the hand going back and forth, back and forth,
So soothing and warming on just the skin behind the clothes.
The girls change, sexually, belly open to the air
And then, later, in age, their buttocks sag, with the clothes.

My father died

When I was little, I was happy as a lark.
I lived in a womb of love and safety.

Then my father died, and in my head
I thought that I was an orphan,
A half of a person, for half of him was me.
I had tried to be like him,
his humor, his joy,
his graciousness.
But I did not mourn,
I hid under a bell jar, and sealed it tight.
I could not release my grief.
For years I was stuck, anxious, nervous,
a half of my self,
my promise withered with my tears and fears.

Then one day, I cried.
And I cried for all the fathers who died too young.
And I cried for all the little girls whose fathers went to an early
    grave.
And the jar opened, and my feelings tumbled out into the world.

But the sadness remained.
Time had ambushed me
letting it get out of hand.
Years and talents were at waste,
and now I must cherish my fragile mind
and keep it safe from stupidity and fate.

Womb of Love

This poem was about my feelings on joining my poetry group.

Womb of Love, finding hate.
I was born in a womb of love.
I never heard a scream of hate.
I never felt a slap of rage,
Only kisses soft as doves.

Now I know the world is cruel,
too late to be prepared.
They did not warn me
for the world we have.

I am an innocent, perhaps, a fool.
I feel the smallest sting,
I want goodness to be near,
And evil breaks my heart.
I have no shield, no barrier,
I am delicate as an anemone,
without a shell.

But now, in this class,
I feel that I am not alone.

My Pillow is my best friend

My pillow is my best friend.
I stroke the soft cotton,
I punch the pillow to make the best fit.
If I lie down, deeply into the bed,
I have a surprise.
My body shrinks like Lilliput,
Or Alice gone astray.
I think I see waving tendrils and filaments,
waving like seaweed, way down in the gulf.

Spring cleaning

Spring cleaning is a time of regeneration.
Spring cleaning is a time of growth,
A time to discard the things we no longer use.
Spring cleaning is a cleansing of the body,
And the cleansing of the spirit and the soul.

At spring cleaning I'm a snake,
casting off my old skin.
And spring cleaning clears more space for the world.
I branch out like trees which burst into flowers,
To welcome a new year, and wipe out the old slate.

In the Pool at the YMCA

In the pool I defy gravity, I lose 200 pounds in a minute.
In the pool my joints soften, flexible,
like a young green sapling, with tender small sprouts.

In the pool, I watch the patterns and ripples from the other
    swimmers.
The ones who kick loudly, creating huge bellows
of bubbles which are so much fun.

Then I turn over on my back, looking up into the sky,
with brilliant swells of billowing clouds.

Then I flick my red goggles, suddenly pale water becomes
    luminous,
gorgeous turquoise, as beautiful as Bruegel's best work.

With another flip of the green goggles,
the color of the water changes back to swim-house blue.

It is time to get out.
My fingers are wrinkled, my hair reeks of chlorine, and gravity
    returns.
Oh! To be light again,
in waters with colors that I can bring back.

Dreams and Reality

Now there is a new thing with my brain
I have dreams that seem real, where I don't have my disease.
I had poems of swimming, and ice skating, and snorkeling.
Now I get confused with poetry and dreams.
If I can feel my truth, and see my world,
I see it as a canal or road.
Yesterday the air was clear,
There were no distractions,
And I felt light like a balloon.
I am coming back to myself, perhaps a little,
And it seems some kind of magic.
I don't expect much, but I will try.
Of course, I want to be cured, and it's impossible.
But I have little moments, so clean and happy.

The following six poems were written when my mother Tillie had a heart attack

My mother may be dying

My mother is dying. Her feet gave in. She falls.
The Paramedics come.

Her heart, her wonderful insightful, loving heart is broken,
gluey with cholesterol and plaques.

She is not waiting for medication to cure her.
She wants to peacefully pass away.
She has been there before, she said. She is not afraid
She came back again
But now she says she is ready to go,
this independent, non-spiritual woman who has seen the light,
the golden light of the tunnel.
She is a true traveler, even to the voyage to Hades,
And she has come back.
But now her own mother is calling her,
She is ready to come back to her own mother too.

This woman, Tillie, my mother,
is the most wonderful person that I will ever know

We honor that. She falls yet again.
Each time she jests with the young medics, flirting,
always cheerful as they do their work.

Finding humor, even with the gallows line swaying in the
breeze.

She falls yet again in her house, wedged between her buffet and
her recliner.
She managed to have a near-lethal fall on the floor.
She always had new ways of doing things.

I walk my ritual exercise.
The crape myrtle outside my window blooms with its bright
pink flowers.
These flowers will be there next year. But my mother will not.
She will not.
She knows she is ready.

Whose heart will be broken? My heart? My daughter's heart?
I turn my head. The bed is empty. She is gone.

The hospital bed

My mother is still in the hospital,
with her white hair sticking out in all directions,
her soft chin doubled with soft rolls of flesh.

She lies in bed peeping over her neck,
tangled up with coiled tubing,
tubing that tells us how her brave heart beats.

Meanwhile I, her daughter,
move from one bed in the house to another,
trying to find a safe haven for her, and for me.

We hardly sleep.

Will she wake up in this bed or not?
Will she lie in coronary care, or intensive care, or be sent home?
Or kept for a while, to wake up in a bed in my house?

She will have her final bed, sometime sooner or later.

And when she comes home,
I, her daughter, will take care of her,
and caress her and love her.

She refuses any invasive tests or procedures.
She says she is ready to go.

Now I sit by her on her hospital bed,.
I hold her and caress her,
like a mother cat licking her kitten.

I pile onto her bed,
and hope that—what?

A soft landing to the last part of her life.

Raising the dead

For those who are raised from the dead,
The world is not quite the same.
The flowers are blooming
But she cannot lean over to smell the sweet rose.

For those who are raised from the dead,
Glimpses of memories are lost.
Blank
What?
Confusion beyond repair, whipped out, zilch.

'Tis a pity, for such a very fine brain.
And I, and this mother of mine, we stand together.
Her problem is a vampire, a loss of pressure
To barely push blood through her body,
And I fight the plaque and tangles of Alzheimer's

How can we cope?
Gone is transportation.
Gone are accurate appointments.
And yet…in the same body, the same values, the same pleasures.
Our family is fragmenting as our body parts decay.
What a strange life we are having now.

The gathering of forces.

Today is the gathering of forces.
Out came the diagnosis of pneumonia.

Who is the enemy? Who will make it well?
Out came the phone book,
Out came the email,
Out come the near family and far.
We will watch, and hug, and caress
Each other, for all of us, and they are us.

Many have been through this before,
But the main player on this stage is Tillie.
She is the hero. She chooses the plot,
The manner of it, in her own way, which we will honor
To our best of our ability. It may be hard.

Several voices, a cacophony of interventions.
All I want to do is lay down on our largest bed,
And hug and stroke each other, and murmuring
Little thoughts, or jokes, and then, when she is ready,
she can fade away.

As Shakespeare said,
"This you perceive, which makes thy love more strong,
To love that well which thou must leave ere long."

The Witching Hour at the Hospital

It is midnight,
The witching hour.
The telephone phone rings. Beelzebub jumps
on to Tillie's shoulders, bringing with it her searing pain.
The infection festers.
She is scared.
In her little girl voice she says,
"Please pick me up
I need to go to the hospital."
I take a big breath. Here we go again.
I worry also, as a daughter and a nurse.
New ooze is still destroying her toe.
I thought we were finally over that.

For me, it is a miserable time, sitting on hard chairs,
No food, no water, and no information.
That's how they treat people here in this E.R.
It's not like it is on TV.
If I were comfortable, treated as a guest
Being there would not have been so disappointing.
Or it would not matter so much,
but all I see are the gossiping nurses, chatting with their peers,
ignoring the patients, even though
the cup of water is only a few feet away.

I am a nurse, and I know what nursing means.
Caring, soothing, listening, learning, serving
But not here.

Finally the x-rays reveal a healing process, thank God, not death,
    this time.
I think she would have been better at home.

Tillie's ducks

Tillie saw her doctors, lined up like ducks
Each found problems,
each found things to do.
We turn around to see the past
and the possible futures.
Now we see it differently,
it is no longer acute, but chronic.
She wanted better circulation,
she wanted less pain.
She refuses to even consider stronger medicine,
or even a wheel chair, if she cannot
move around herself.
She is in the "I'll never use that" mode.
Just like the pacemaker,
that she welcomes to save her life.
She's not stupid, but she is stubborn.
She'll do what she needs to do.

Well, the foot is still with Dr Shelly.
He is a red haired man who touches
Tillie's feet with gentleness and caring:
I wish that other doctors would be so solicitous.

Now she tries her other podiatry shoes, wiggling,
Finding a way to avoid pain.

My Husband

My Roger
My husband
He loves me incredibly
And we have good sex.
My husband Roger is a very strong person.
His arms are strong, and sometimes press me too hard.
But, he lives the life of man.
He is The Man.
Unfortunately, I'm rather delicate in both mind and touch.
He might not like it, but so what?
Roger loves me very deeply.
I find myself trying to use his brain.
He likes to be fast
And he has a wonderful brain!
It's like a computer, an encyclopedia, a resource library!
When he starts anything, it's like a zzsszzeeeeiii!
Roger loves women, beautiful or not, small or rotund
and he treats all of them with kindness.
Roger says proudly—he wants to have a baby!
He wants the feeling of the baby, the experience.

My Roger
My Husband
With you, I fell like we are each other,
Like there is no separation between our cells,
Our lives so intertwining,
Moving with and between one another,
Over and over and over and always.

Roger's Gradebooks

So I stumbled through my day,
Cleaning things behind bookshelves,
Finding cobwebs and yellowed old receipts.

Then I found papers from Roger, my husband,
Of his gradebooks when he was a boy.
I won't do anything until he sees them.

There are also photos,
Faded photos of people I never knew.

Perhaps he will find a smidgen of sentimentality in his soul
When he sees the faded papers,
And faded photos, and gradebooks.

Or, maybe not.
He protects his stuff,
But never looks at the piles of faded lives.

That's how the piles come,
Faded old magazines and newspapers,
And magazines with slippery shiny paper
That yearn to slide to the floor.

He is ambivalent about this,
A danger for his privacy,
But he sighs with pleasure
When an old treasure is found.

The Ice Skater

I am obsessed with ice skating.

In my dreams
and in my body,
I am an ice skater, flowing across the ice.
My hair flows behind me, like silk.
My legs are strong, my thighs tight, I go faster and faster in my
    spin.
I can stop on a dime, with my slim strong arms.
I am in heaven.
I feel like an angel,
with wings that carry me out of this world.
I check the TV guide for the ice skating programs,
I drop everything else,
I am obsessed.

Once upon a time, I could run and jump, and even skate, a little.
I found that I could feel those remarkable jumps.
My love of the sport is so intense,
My body becomes the skater, in my mind,
Where there are no falls, where I jump and twirl, and fly across
    the stadium,
and I sway and move and shift my body with the music,
and I move with my body's knowledge.
I heave breaths of exhaustion, even the tiredness after the
    program.

I can feel the skate, and by the end of the day, I'm exhausted,
as if my body is here, exultant, ready for the prize.

The noisy ladies

I am sad.
I am surrounded by intelligent women.
They are very vocal,
Their thoughts dance in their brains.
I am no dancer now, with words that go blank.
And then there is a noise,
A bombardment from every side.
My head explodes with pieces,
fragments and shards of fine ideas
That don't reach beyond a child's world.
Hiding behind there is a small, quiet place,
One that gives me a road to travel
With the love of my family who read my ideas for me.
I am a writer,
when my emotions sing, and thoughts come forth.
With a little push from my husband,
I delete bad grammar, and with his help
I can find the essence of my thoughts
When I write from the essence of my soul.

My dreams

I dream with details, with color, movement and even body
  language.
I wonder how this is, for a person who has lost her words.
The dreams roll on like any writing.
I use the computer like anyone else.
I don't know how I can do this.
The dreams are like plays that
I might write tomorrow.
Frequently I am filled with wondrous words.

What is the brain that is doing this miracle?
If I talk in the dream my speech is fluent, and the words are
  there.
I would like to ask a neurologist how this happens.
In the daze of half-sleep my brain seems whole,
And in my dreams it is the source of poetry.
Even in a noisy environment, it can have wisps of clarity, quick,
  clean.

Christmas Slippers

I survived Christmas. Oops, what about my slippers?
Last year they were beginning to fray
I have nostalgia about these slippers.
They are red plaid, which I find cheerful.
I held on for a long time, years, it seems
For the slippers to decay.
Now, my toe has stuck out of the slipper.
I look at the slippers again.
Red, fluffy, I feel like I am holding
my childhood "blankie", which I no longer have.
These are the slippers that have warmed my feet
For so many years.

Now I must get new ones,
With hope, health and happiness.

Fairies

This morning something happened in my little study.
I was still muggy with getting dressed.
Something was a little different
And the room became radiant
With dancing motes swirling around in a little tornado,
As reflection glared from something that I had not seen before.
The little tornado whisked in one direction and another
And blew away.

I knew how this happened.
The full moon at night was so bright,
And it was fairy time.
Not often do we play with fairies,
But this seemed real.
The music, the dancing, the twinkles and reflections.
It was Fairy Time.

Noise and beauty

Noise and beauty in my room.
At first the house was quiet, with intermissions.
Then the gardeners were blowing the leaves,
A huge sound that can ruin my ears.
The next sound was better, but also very loud, one of music.
There is a strange thing that noises are so different,
From the delicate tinkle of a tiny stream,
To the plane going by, washing the sky with sound.
And Mozart's great organ tones,
from such a small and brilliant young man.
Meanwhile I hear the computer hiss in the background
And the clicks of the keyboard,
While crockery clinks and clatters in the kitchen.
While I hear another music, Telemann this time.
In this house I am surrounded with music,
from Bach to Beethoven to the Beatles.

Brain and gut

I honor the love of my family and friends,
Who love me and cherish me no matter what.
   Later it may become difficult,
   When people will need to wipe up my parts.

I can appreciate nature, and its beauty and grace.
I can not love my body, which has betrayed me before.
I must love my brain, even as I watch it float away.
   The mind tries to heal the brain,
   I find it scrambled, my brain taking my mind from me.

But I am still here, thick wads of gunk around my gut.
I feel that I am strangling, a python around my waist.
   Now there are hopes for travel, for delight

But I'm afraid that the coils of plaques and tendrils are stronger
      then me,
and my mind, which watches, in despair,
the brain and the gut, both in a state of degeneration,
where the only way left is down.

In the gut, I feel choked with despair
How can I breath?
How can I eat?
How can I open myself to the air, with those coils around my
      gut?

Now, maybe, Shakespeare will distract me.
   Teaching may help me get me off the hook .

Yes, it may work, for a while
I feel my head is like fluff, slow to respond, even doing the easiest
    things.

Maybe Shakespeare will work, and be my redeemer
    Now with my love of work, my love with my pal Bill,
    Who may be my redeemer.

A slower life

Tillie keeps on her routine:
Medicines, various nurses,
and all of them treat her like a queen.
That is how our lives are going.

Tillie has pain, and I am pained by my loss of words.
How can I cope?
I live in a world of sensations, music, walking.
My world is full of movement, touching, smells.
That is what I thrive in: I need the wind, and the music.
My life now is free of all the wars,
and debates, and confrontations.
I always wanted to keep that stuff away.
So, my life is what I want to know,
with friends, and fine animals,
and I don't need to talk very much.
I have dreams in my head in full knowledge
Of all I need to know.
My people and my friends
can fit in the words that I need.
I am content to be slower
with my garden, in a slower world.

Losses

I lost autonomy

I lost independency

I lost words

I lost transportation

I lost spelling

I lost certainty

I lost delight

I lost jokes

I lost comics

I lost time

I lost space

I lost quickness

I lost a future

I lost a beautiful brain

I have love

I have animals

I have food

I have good friends

I have respect

I have health

I have swimming

I have the sun and sky

I have music

I have walks

I can still read

I can still write

I am still here

Learning New Words

All of these new words begin with "A"
This is not good news
The "A" refers to an absence,
A blank,
A bother for others, trying to find the words,
For I am trapped in a cage of tendrils and plaques.

I was a wordsmith, joyous with language
I am left with others to give me my words.
Now, I gesture, like a blind person.

A is for aphasia, the inability to find words
A is for amnesia, inability to remember
A is for aphonia, inability to speak
A is for apraxia, inability to make words
A is for Aricept, a medicine that may work
A is for attention, so I do not forget
A is for Alzheimer's, that rips out my soul

Lost words

No words that I make see it.
The words mean nothing,
The words dead end.
A black hiss there is the words when
My love for writing
Hits my lost skill of touch-typing
And the words are broken
Never to return whole.

Anger

I am so angry at my disabilities that I hurt,
And when I get angry, I back out of things.
Like the keyboard, which I should practice,
but no, I stupidly back off, and feel despair.
This is the Laurel who was so proactive.
Now I curl in a ball like my cat.

This is a time of losses.
JAG on TV, with its fine ideals, is ending.
And I must give my garden work a break,
as my wrist is in pain,
and I must pick up and tidy away the debris
and some big piles of sticks and dead leaves.
And with all that work,
I have one beautiful red flower that dies.
I'm sad a lot these days.
It's the love of my family that keeps me going.

Despair of Alzheimer's

I had such a wonderful world,
Surrounded by excellence.
Now I can't make a phone call,
Now I need help to put on my clothes.
Now I have no independence.
I'm like Alice, in a topsy world,
saying the wrong word,
All from this disease.

I am still lucid in my brain, but only in my dreams.
When I wake, my aphasia rips out the words.

I love flowers, the smells, the morning birdsongs.
The flowers are a pleasure but I seem to kill them.
One bright deep purple flower is so sturdy, it keeps going on,
Like my mother Tillie, so strong.
But I am in another world, silent with grief.

Aphasia

To my surprise, I have the words in my head.
When I read, I read the words as my first wonder and joy.
I was supposed to know only black holes in my brain.
In fact I know all the words,
despite the aphasia that constantly grows.
Is it true? Is it?
I have worked hard to get this.
I have aphasia, the loss of words.
But they didn't really go away.
How I do it?
Exercise of the body and the brain.
I do not let my disabilities strangle me.
As the neurologists say, I have such material in my brain.
I think there are others like me,
Who refuse to lose ourselves.
These are the heroes who refuse to give in.
Assert mind over brain, and keep the mind intact.

Little Expectations

Now I have little expectations.
I work in the joy of the garden.
I found that plants do not go fast,
And they do not make me feel the pain
Of the horrors of these days.
I feel the quiet of the trees and birds.
I know that I will be getting smaller, and not think of this.
It is a reprieve of my work and life,
And with my disease I will be free,
Because I will no longer be in the turmoil of hate, and terror,
And with my lovely family I will just go away.

Thanks

One is for Dan,
Then for the cat,
Then for my daughter,
Then there is the garden,
And now the music—classical music—
And the wind,
And colors, best with red and gold.

This is such a very small set of precious things.
Now, all of these things are necessary.
This family, my friends, and the stars
And jewels of thoughts
which sing in my dreams.

Beethoven's Pastoral Symphony

Today I wanted to be happy
And I listened to Beethoven's Pastoral Symphony
I loved the twitters of birds, and the chirps,
And I could even smell the flowers.
The music is so sweet,
the swelling and the breadth of that movement,
then the bursts of joy.

Now I don't have to do anything.
But I don't like life like that.
I had such a life of the mind, so sad
Now it is gone forever.
But I will keep my sweet soul
And still listen to Beethoven.

Facing Alzheimer's

The following essay, on my experience so far with Alzheimer's disease, and on my prospects, was one of my last prose works before I turned to writing poetry

The first time I knew I had a problem was when I got lost on a corner of two streets I knew very well. I looked one way and another, and didn't know which way to go. I immediately self-diagnosed myself, so I could avoid denial, and have time to figure out what to do. Although my 86-year-old mother has no mental deficits, my aunt had suffered from Alzheimer's Disease (AD), so there was a genetic factor which made me suspect the worst.

Two years earlier, I had co-written a medical mystery. In one chapter, I created a character, a judge, who loses his way on a downtown street, and luckily one of his colleagues finds the judge disoriented and confused, and takes him home. In my own mind, I thought I knew how it would feel to have AD. Now I felt that my fictional character and his behavior had been accurate: this is how it feels to be a person with Alzheimer's Disease.

For me, as a writer, scholar, and lover of music and the arts, my loss of memory was catastrophic. I was very smart person, top of the class, with five degrees, and a brain filled with libraries of books, travels and adventure, insights, and deep ideas, often prophetic. I was witty and quick, delightful in conversation, caring with others. I loved having two careers, one in literature, and the other in nursing and medicine. My field was Medical Humanities, and I taught the psycho-social aspects of health care at a prestigious university.

This episode of confusion was a warning sign which showed up rarely at first, and I was functioning essentially normally. But when my husband was diagnosed with prostate cancer, I emotionally collapsed.

Then I was asked to resign three of my jobs. First the nursing went, because I couldn't quickly handle the medications, then the Medical Humanities job was lost, because my insight was poor, and then the addiction job became exhausting, and I could not stay alert and thoughtful for ten hours at a time. This left only a part-time job teaching writing and literature, which I can still handle. I tried some home nursing, but I had trouble with going to people's houses, finding their addresses, and keeping my paperwork straight.

It was about this time that my husband (who had had successful surgery) and I faced up to the reality that I was probably in an early stage of Alzheimer's. We tried to find every possible disease that has symptoms of cognitive deficits, from Lyme Disease to Major Depression, that was not Alzheimer's. But everything pointed to early Alzheimer's.

My mother is a nurse, and my husband tracks many of the sciences and new technologies, with subscriptions to *Nature* and *Science* and other scientific journals, and I subscribe to the *Journal of the American Medical Association* and the *New England Journal of Medicine*. For both of us, the brain is the most important organ in the body. With all this information, I prepared myself to confront my memory problems head on.

As a writer, I am sensitive to the connotations of words, and how powerful they could be.

Naming the disease was horrific. I had only a few words to use: dementia, organic brain disorder, senility, and Alzheimer's. I was obviously not demented, or senile, or having an organic brain disorder, at least based on my functioning now.

With a few words, "probable early onset Alzheimer's," my world was turned around. It was a catastrophe. How could I be a person with Alzheimer's? In a wide range of situations I still feel physically and mentally fine. But the word *dementia* hurt me the most. My identity could not be "dementia". That is for old ladies in convalescent homes, not this lively, intelligent, person who teaches at a university. But the words, "probable early onset Alzheimer's" was like a shot in my chest, and I fell, fighting and screaming (quietly) into anger and despair, and at that single moment I lost my sense of self. I let the words take over my identity, and it has taken quite a while to gradually find myself again.

From my knowledge of disease processes, I know that almost all disorders are on a continuum, including lethal disorders like plague and AIDS. I felt I belonged somewhere along the continuum. I have problems with my short-term memory, but also I still have memory for a wide range of categories, from designing gourmet food to recognition of people's body language, and still have fast reflexes and a wide range of skills and functioning.

I felt there must be a name for people who function well, with some deficits, and without dementia. So I felt vindicated when there was an announcement of a new diagnostic classification: Mild Cognitive Impairment (MCI). In this disorder, the first symptom of which is memory loss, there is a risk for Alzheimer's in the future. Meanwhile, the person lives a normal life, with fewer deficits than Alzheimer's patients, but more deficits than normal controls.

To be pro-active in my neurological health, I accessed the educational materials available from the Alzheimer's Association. The information from the Association was excellent, especially on coping skills which may retard the speed of degeneration. In fact, the materials would be appropriate for any person with any medical or neurological problem.

I also found three books helpful: *There's Still a Person in There: The Complete Guide to Treating and Coping with Alzheimer's* by Michael Castelman, Dolores Gallagher-Thompson, Ph.D. and Matthew Naythons, MD; *Brain Longevity* by Dharma Singh Khalsa, MD; and *Perfect Health: The Complete Mind/Body Guide* by Deepak Chopra, MD.

Besides my subscriptions to the two leading medical journals, I spend time on the Web catching up with Alzheimer's research and obesity research, another unexpected epidemic, and I took out free subscriptions to the *Alzheimer Research Forum Newsletter, Medscape's Neurology Medpulse,* and the National Institute on Aging's newsletter on Alzheimer's Disease Research. I found that progress in Alzheimer's research has been accelerating, and there is even hope for a cure with the new vaccine, which cleared up the plaques and produced improvements in mental functioning in mice.

I also studied alternative medicine, as well as the Western model of care. I have always been interested in Wellness models of healing. Actually, I don't have much of a choice: a bio-chemical gate-keeper in my body seems to think that supplements are toxic, and my body blows out these medications with violent diarrhea.

But there is also the body healing itself. In repeated studies of cognition in rats, those which are stimulated have heavier brains than normal rats; and even in adult rats, the neurons in the hippocampus area can make new dendrites under the stimulation of new tasks and environments. A study of London taxi drivers, who have to spend at least two years intensively learning the geography of London, also showed neuronal growth in the relevant area in the brain.

Studies on rats indicate that rats in stimulating environments, which I call the Disneyland rats, do better than sedentary ordinary rats in their cages. The Disneyland rats had new cages and games every day. When the brains of the Disneyland rats were autopsied, the Disneyland rats had larger brains than before, while the ordinary rats degenerated at their usual rate.

So I decided to live like a very stimulated rat. I decided that this would be the model for my treatment plan: Stimulation, stimulation, stimulation. I am on the computer writing every day, and reading scientific journals, and talking with interesting people, and swimming laps in the pool, and playing computer games that are made to tease the brain. Or I'm on the Internet findings focusing on other diseases, Mad Cow, Ebola, Foot and Mouth disease. We seem to be surrounded by fascinating diseases. And I read the latest progress with Alzheimer's and other kinds of disease. Studies show behavioral interventions do seem to work, and a low fat diet, anti-oxidant foods, exercise, social support, and mental stimulation, are always available, at no cost. I take to heart that advice.

Now new games are available that enhance brain stimulation. One of them on the market is "ThinkFast", a game which is supposed to help exercise the brain for physical reflexes, subliminal awareness, instinctive thinking, decision making, and working memory. The computer tracks the player's progress, and charts help the player discover how the brain is working. I notice that if I neglect the game for a while, my scores go down, which I can see on the screen. But if I play regularly, I get unexpected peaks of high scores. This encourages me: it really does exercise the brain. ThinkFast indicates that I have been fairly stable. I don't get better, but stability rather than cure is my goal.

I also have an EEG biofeedback setup in my home, in the form of an extra PC with electrodes attached, which I use for about 25 minutes nearly every day. (See the book *A Symphony in the Brain* by Jim Robbins) My husband attaches electrodes to my skull, and I try to achieve healthy brain wave patterns, with rewards using a maze, or using a pattern like watching the wake of a boat. The theory suggests that when the brain is in balance, memory, thinking, and focus can improve. We are not expecting any kind of cure, but the treatment does seem to make me feel more physically and mentally comfortable, and even happy. I don't know if the biofeedback works, but it does no harm, and the stimulation of the brain may be helping to slow its deterioration.

I am still able to function adequately as a part-time English teacher at a small supportive college, and my last student evaluations were above the faculty average. My knowledge of literature is intact, and my writing is still good as long as I can use a keyboard, but my use of pen and pencil is poor. I was assigned classes that are scheduled for the evening. My husband drives, because I can't make long freeway trips at night, with the glare of the headlights and my inability to see spaces between cars

Meanwhile, at the college, I have started noticing students who have their own deficits, such as stress, memory loss, forgetfulness, lack of focus, and confusion. As a nurse, I can help them integrate their own psychiatric and neurological problems with their academic needs. We are all in this together, and they appreciate my ability to understand their problems so well. In fact, when I was talk to my colleagues, we remark about how our students have the same problems. Their levels of cognition are lower, they have trouble with abstract issues, they look exhausted, have poor concentration, have bouts of confusion and problems tracking. I am not suggesting that college students are at risk of dementia, but we now have a culture which includes drug use, eating disorders, and tremendous stress.

I have discovered that when one of my deficits occurs, it takes a while for the family to get used to my losses, including help that I need from them. Transportation is the most important problem, but I can get to the YMCA pool nearby. I cannot drive at night: there is a terrible glare combined with a spatial problem if I try to shift lanes, which I find too scary. So far, however, I can negotiate my trip to the YMCA pool, and I recognize places within four miles of my home. If necessary, I drive around until I hit a familiar landmark, and then I simply go home.

Since I am semi-retired, I've been going to movies. I've discovered it isn't as easy as it used to be. Reading the print that designates the movie house, and the time of the show gets all scrambled with my eyes, with the miniscule print. Then with my short-term memory problems, I forget which movie house I need to attend. Was it the UA at 12 noon or was it Century 8 at 3:15? To ensure getting the movie times right, I come early, and I have a higher probability of getting the right show. Getting these things right is frustrating, which makes me sad and irritable.

I am also having different kinds of problems with movies. The sound is horribly noisy for me, and I sat through one very exciting movie pressing my ear lobes to cut down the noise. And then there is the content of the movie. At this time in my life, I am not interested in violent fast-moving objects screeching through the sky. But I can have trouble with quiet movies as well. I seem to view the film in a passive superficial way, and if the plot is complex, I really don't understand the nuances of the story. Foreign movies with subtitles are almost impossible, trying to do two things at once. Nevertheless, I go to movies, as part of my regime of cognitive stimulation.

One of my tricks is to push ahead no matter what. If there is a deficit, I take charge. I attack that word, or complete the idea, and I bring myself back to baseline. I decide to go out. When things are difficult I attack the problem as best I can. I refuse to be depressed. Sometimes tiredness does hold me back from action, but then, I think that my job is to take a nap, and take care of myself, and enjoy the sweetness of lying down and feeling the pillow and the bed, pressing against my body. That is lovely as well.

I don't officially meditate, but I pay attention to the world, I smell that beautiful rose, I hear the piece of music, I stretch up to the sky, waving my hands, and watching my shadow sway in the wind.

My husband decided that he should take me to Paris and Italy, while I was coherent and able to have a good time. They were wonderful trips. My whole body and soul absorbed the arts and music and countryside and food, and it was marvelous. Since my map-reading skills have completely gone, my husband had to keep an eye on me. Once in Paris my husband jumped into the Metro train to get a seat, and the doors closed behind him before I could get on. I decided the best thing to do was to stay exactly where I was. To keep myself calm, rather than anxious, I looked around my environment. There was a young man with a guitar, and the people seemed harmless, and after about 20 minutes my husband came back for me. But this was not easy for me. I felt anxious, and abandoned, and unsure of myself.

We have continued to have short trips, during my husband's days off. And we had another long overseas trip, full of love and laughter with our friends and relatives. But again, things were not perfect. One symptom of this disease is a problem with balance as well as problems with space and time. We were in a museum, descending stairs in low lighting—another thing that doesn't work for people with this disorder. Put the two together, and I badly sprained my right foot. From then on, I was using a cane, which I had to remember to use, and not to forget and leave it at the house. Instead, I had pain, and the out-of-balance feeling my body has when using a cane reinforces my problems with mobility. I have a high risk for falls. I developed an intimate relationship with various cars, and would hold onto parts of the car's body, as I climbed in and out of these small spaces to get into driveways and cars. Every day as I untangle myself from the belts and buttons, it reminds me how in the past I could glide through the world, in balance. My mind and body were one, but now, each part of me, the car, the curbs, the cane, the belts, all seem to be out to hurt me.

Based on my personal experience, as well as research, medicines do not yet work well on Alzheimer's. Aricept and perhaps other medications have a short life of helpfulness. Meanwhile research sites all over the world are working with new medicines which might work with one person, if not for another. Every now and then I try one of the supplements that supposedly can help memory. Each time, my body squirts out the pills with explosive diarrhea. The safest program would be based on ordinary foods, exercise, and social support. I have read work on nutrients, especially anti-oxidants, and folic acid for the brain and heart, and vitamin E. I have been eating blueberries since reading a study from Tufts University in which blueberries produced improvement in memory in elderly rats; this was attributed to the antioxidant effect of the blueberries' phytochemicals. I prefer my vitamin C with fresh fruits, not pills.

One aspect of Alzheimer's research seems to be missing: who is studying people who do well? Are there people who by their behavior, environment, or genetics, do well, and are able to slow down their degeneration? I hope to be one of those people. Now I look forward to a time when Alzheimer's is just another treatable chronic disorder. We need to find the remedy as fast as possible, because the Baby Boomers are waiting in line. Alzheimer's will join AIDS in being recognized as an epidemic, as the Baby Boomers over 60 start down the path, one they never thought would happen, wrecking their hopes for a vigorous and joyous retirement. I have tracked AIDS, and now I will track AD, and it isn't a pretty picture. But AIDS can lead the way, regarding medication, research, caretaking, social support, and the various needs which will be revealed.

I am still very loath to reveal my disorder, for several reasons. I found out that if I mention the "A" word, it creates emotional pain that I wouldn't want to put on anybody. Right now, AD is like the old problem of the taboo on mentioning cancer. The word means a death sentence, and I am nowhere near that. And we now know that AD has many different levels of functioning, just as HIV has levels of deterioration. Many HIV positives have stayed with HIV and never progressed to full blown AIDS. Alzheimer's is the end stage of my disease, while MCI (Mild Cognitive Impairment) is in the middle somewhere, with hope for treatments.

Instead of saying I have Alzheimer's, I can use simple unthreatening words. "I have a problem with memory sometimes." "I have a spatial problem." "My eyes are giving me trouble today." And I ask for help: yesterday I asked the checker to fill in my check, which she did without a blink.

The next usual step would be to go to an Alzheimer's support group, for support and education. We felt that we had enough of that, and we have the resources with us all the time. I did have several phone conversations about Alzheimer's issues, and found the staff charming, compassionate, knowledgeable and hopeful. But at this stage people find me normal and healthy, and then the person can't believe that I may have Alzheimer's. A few days ago I talked on the phone to a work colleague whom I hadn't heard from for a year, and who knows my diagnosis. She said that in her opinion, I was just the same bright quick person that she knows. Which was true—we had a great time talking, not chitchat, but discussion of issues in the workplace, and values, and knowledge. But if she had asked me what day it was, I would have been a blank.

I follow the suggestions of Andrew Weil, M.D. and the Wellness programs. I rely on their advice about nutrition, exercise, sleep hygiene, laughter, and all the other behaviors that stimulate the brain and make the soul happy. These coping skills are available from the Alzheimer's Association, which has excellent materials for people at all states of the illness.

I have cleared off unnecessary people, tasks, and behaviors. I have lifted burdens off my shoulder. I have followed the suggestions of 12-step programs, regarding letting go, and letting things happen, which they have. I am here, alive and well.

My swimming routine is a combination of meditation in the soothing water, and good full body exercise for strength. We also take walks in the woods: nature, the water and sky, and the trees are also healing.

Classical music may be good for the brain (the "Mozart effect"), and I feel that it heals the soul; we have classical music on most of the time. I try to envelop my brain in a continuous world of cognition, aesthetics, beauty, music, movement, and joy.

Whenever I find myself with a deficit, I try to deal with it immediately (before I forget). For example, I have a specific place for the keys (everybody knows about that!) If I find my eyes doing weird things with spatial relationships, I sit down and play with the spatial patterns, so that I, and not the neurology, am controlling it. The same thing with the numb fingertips, a symptom I discovered quite a long while ago. Now when I twiddle my thumbs, I am exercising the fingertips.

Meanwhile, my body also has gastric problems. I have to be very careful about what I eat, as I believe that diarrhea is not good for the brain, as all those nutrients are washed away. Sometimes when my irritable bowel is in action, I have had episodes of real exhaustion, so I allow myself a nap, which really turns into watching interesting things on the TV. Basically I have my mind and body engaged almost around the clock. And so far I sleep well, and live well, most of the time.

I have bouts of lack of initiative. I have to distinguish between having a good reason for not wanting to do something, and "I'm tired, I don't want to go to that movie." One of my support people drags me there, and I have a good time.

Some of the deficits do not want to change. I have calendars, but the brain doesn't recognize what I should do. I have lost arithmetic, so I use a calculator. I also find filling out forms very difficult: the lines and blocks seem to dance around.

Word loss is an increasing problem. But I can be patient for the word to show up. Or I find synonyms, or talk around the topic. Our household is very verbal people, with mediocre non-verbal language skills. It can be hard for them to understand my waving hands, but they try to supply the word I'm looking for.

Basically I work hard at all this. It is not easy to do something you don't want to do. It is not easy to be patient about words and thoughts. It is not easy to live with a brain that no longer functions as well as it should. It is not easy to know that for me this will be the end of the road.

I can think about myself at this time in several ways.

I can think that I remain, for the most part, normal, and avoid those areas which I cannot do. I could think that the scimitar of Alzheimer's is over my head. Or, I can say, I should fully live every day.

My aunt Gertie was a smart business woman, and she ran several stores for quite a long time. I don't know when her Alzheimer's showed up. I do know that she became very reclusive, but she was always a loner, somewhat strange, and very independent. She did not invite people to her tiny apartment, and owned only the bare necessities for living. She also had the habit of giving away any gifts that someone would give to her.

Do I think she was altruistic? Or maybe she wanted to live with almost monastic simplicity? She was a gentle person, and whenever we visited her, which was not very welcome, she was concerned that I should have children. When we last visited her, she had got to the level of few words repeated over and over: "Does Laurel have children, does Laurel have children?" We reassured her, over and over, knowing that her short-term memory was gone, and she had to ask the question again and again.

She refused treatment for her lung and tissue cancer. Now I know why she did that: to avoid the degeneration of Alzheimer's and a horrible death. She got her wish. She died while eating breakfast, according to the staff, though they were pretty vague about it. They suggested it was a heart attack, which was not unlikely with her family history of heart attacks. Or she may have choked on her food, or aspirated food and died of aspiration pneumonia. Nowadays I think about what kind of death is waiting for me. A gentle one, I hope.

978-0-595-40885-0
0-595-40885-0

Made in the USA
Las Vegas, NV
02 October 2021